Recipe Book for I. C. Interstitial Cystitis

By

E. Murphy
Assisted by
Mr J. G. Murphy BSc (Hons) DIP
Emergency Care Practitioner

Pen Press Publishers Ltd.

© E. Murphy 2007

First published in Great Britain by
Pen Press Publishers Ltd
The Old School
39 Chesham Road
Brighton BN2 1NB

ISBN: 1-905621-79-5
ISBN13: 978-1-905621-79-8

Printed and bound in the UK

A catalogue record of this book is available from
the British Library

Cover design by Jacqueline Abromeit

Introduction

My book is based on tried and tested foods, by me, over a number of years and have found to be the most tolerated foods for people with Interstitial Cystitis.

They are also very simple and easy to follow recipes for one or two people.

Using only fresh food which is a very healthy diet for all people as it is high in protein energy and low in carbohydrate.

Good luck and best wishes to all.

Eileen Murphy

The Complete Guide to Healthy Eating

This book is for people diagnosed with Interstitial Cystitis advocating high energy foods, high protein food and low in cholesterol.

- Concentrate only on fresh meat, vegetables and fruit.

- With no salt or very low salt – no additives or preservatives.

Especially for people with a medical problem who require such a diet, or for anyone who would like a healthy diet of eating only **fresh meat and vegetables**.

Help and advice on things to avoid such as...

- Salt (sodium), peppers, tomato, vinegar, ready made sauces, most tinned and pre-packed foods have salt and preservatives in them which give the product a longer shelf life, must be avoided especially people diagnosed with I.C.

- This will help stop the painful flare ups, suffered from time to time and enable us to control the pain to keep it to a minimum level.

So, after years of eating anything we like, we now have to re-educate ourselves by watching what we eat and reading labels on packets to maintain a healthy balanced diet and to cope with every day Living when suffering from Interstial Systitus.

Avoid: Ham and hard cheeses.

No: Citric food such as -
Lemon, orange, grapefruit, plums, rhubarb, pineapple etc...

No: dark chocolate (White chocolate okay)

Liquids

> Tea – Decaf
> Coffee – Decaf
> Peppermint tea is good
>
> Water – drink plenty especially before and after meals.

No: alcohol or smoking

No: Cranberry juice

No: Spicy food
(If it burns your stomach it's possible it will burn your bladder.)

No: Sodas
Of any type, especially cola's.

But! Don't be afraid to try different food as long as it is fresh.

Food that is fine to eat and that is well tolerated :

(Fresh Only)
Chicken
Beef
Lamb
Veal
Fish
Cauliflower
Turnip
Broccoli
Beetroot
Carrot
Cabbage
Garden Pea's
Lettuce
Celery
Tomato (home grown)
Salad onion (only if cooked well)
Soft cheeses
Milk cream yoghurt (plain)
Butter
Pasta
Macaroni
Rice
Bread brown or white

Food to stay away from:

Sauces (ready made)
Peppers
Vinegar
Salt (sodium)
Pickled or spicy food
Salad cream
Jam (citric)
Citric fruit
(Lemon, orange, tangerine, cranberry, apple, strawberry, rhubarb, gooseberry, fennel, chillies, sweet and sour marina)
Soda's (especially cola)
Pork products (Bacon,sausage, liver pate, pre-packed cooked meat, pork pie, ham etc...)

No: Additives or preservatives. Always read labels.

Index

Weights and Measures

Approx.

1 oz = 28 gm	3 lb = 1.3 kg
2 oz = 50 gm	6 lb = 2.7 kg
3 oz = 85 gm	10 lb = 4.5 kg
4 oz = 125 gm	
5 oz = 150 gm	
6 oz = 175 gm	

Cooking Time

Gas 1 = 275°F = 135°C
Gas 2 = 300°F = 150°C
Gas 3 = 325°F = 165°C
Gas 4 = 350°F = 180°C
Gas 5 = 375°F = 190°C
Gas 6 = 400°F = 200°C

Liquid

¼ Pint = 150 ml
½ Pint = 275 ml
¾ Pint = 425 ml
1 Pint = 575 ml
1¼ pint = 725ml
1½ pint = 825ml

Linear

20 cm = 8" inch

Homemade Soups

These can be made using fresh stock from beef or chicken when pot roasted.

They also can be kept frozen in ice cube trays for up to one month, to enable us to have freshly made soup with fresh vegetables at any time.

And you can add your favourite fresh herbs, cream and croutons

Minestrone Soup

1 onion (if tolerated) cook well
1 stick of celery
1 pint of beef stock (homemade)
a handful of dry spaghetti

Peel and finely chop the onion, simmer gently for 10 mins in a pan with a lid. Chop and dice the celery, add to the onion, cook for 2 mins.

Pour in the beef stock and simmer for 30 mins.

Break up the spaghetti into one inch pieces then add to the soup and cook for a further 5 mins.

Serve up with crusty bread.

Courgette and Potato Soup

2 courgettes (chopped ½" cube)
1 large potato (diced)
1 medium onion (chopped)
¼ pint milk
1 pint chicken stock (homemade)
A little butter or oil to cook onion

Fry the onion for 5 mins then add the courgette and potato. Stir well and add the stock, milk and simmer for 30 to 35 mins.

Liquidise the soup, return to heat.

Serve up with a swirl of cream and wholemeal roll.

Chicken Soup

1 small onion (chopped) if tolerated
1 large potato (diced)
1 carrot (diced)
1 pint chicken stock (homemade)
Any left over chicken may be used

If using fresh chicken pieces, fry off for 5 mins to seal. Then place in the oven to cook for 5 or 6 mins. Add the potato - and chicken if leftovers - also add the carrot and the stock. Simmer gently for 40 mins.

Serve up with some crusty bread.

Great as a light lunch or supper dish.

Lamb Cutlets

2 lamb cutlets
1 lb potato
6 oz green beans
2 sprigs rosemary
1 tbsp oil

Pan fry the lamb in an oven proof pan for 5 mins to brown and seal with the rosemary and oil.

Then place in a hot oven for 10 mins – gas mark 5 = 375°F.

Peel, chop and boil the potato for 10 mins until cooked. Cream with a knob of butter.

Top and tail the green beans and cook for 5 mins.

Pot Roast Beef

2 lb beef
2 lb potato
1 large carrot
Small cauliflower

Pot roast the beef in an oven proof dish with lid to keep all the flavour in. Add a cup of water and cook for 1½ hours basting once or twice during the cooking time gas mark 5.

Half an hour before the meat is cooked, wash dry and cut the potato into quarters. Peel and quarter the carrot, brush with a little oil onto an oven tray and cook along with the meat.

Chop and prepare the cauliflower into florets and cook for 10 mins. Dish up pouring a little of the beef stock over the dish.

Freeze any remaining stock.

Batter for Yorkshire Pudding

100 gm flour (self raising)
1 large egg
250 ml milk and water (half each)

Sieve the flour into a basin, make a well in the centre, add the egg plus half the liquid and beat well until smooth, then add the rest of the liquid.

Allow the batter to rest for half an hour in a cool place.

Preheat the oven to gas mark 6. Place a tablespoon of oil into each Yorkshire pudding well, and heat up in the oven for 5 mins.

Bring the tray out and just over half fill each one with the batter mixture, cook for about 40 mins until puffed up and crispy.

Chicken and Sauté Vegetables

1 large chicken breast
1 carrot
broccoli
oil for cooking

Pan fry the breast in a little oil for 15 to 20 mins (turning halfway through the cooking.)

Peel and chop the carrot and cook for about 15 mins.

Chop the broccoli into florets, strain the carrot water off and stir fry with the broccoli in a little oil for 5 mins.

Chicken with Rice

1 chicken breast
1 cup of rice
garden peas – handful to garnish
1 pint chicken stock (homemade)

Dice the chicken breast and stir fry in a little oil for 8 to 10 mins.

Cook the rice in the chicken stock or boiling water – bring to boil and simmer for about 8 mins with the lid on the pan.

Cook the garden peas in boiling water for 3 mins.

Serve up the chicken on the bed of rice and garnish with the peas.

Pasta with Cheese Sauce

Pasta shells or twists
1 oz butter
1 oz flour
1 cup of milk
2 oz cheese (grated low salt)
1 tsp oregano

Place the pasta in a pan of boiling water and cover, simmer for 5 to 8 mins.

In a small pan, place the butter over a low heat, add the flour and milk, whisk until smooth and creamy texture.

Cook for 5 mins to cook the flour, then add the grated cheese. Simmer for 1 min.

Strain the pasta and plate up pouring over the cheese sauce sprinkle on some oregano for extra flavour.

Pasta

275 gm or 10 oz flour
2 eggs
2 egg yolks
1 tbsp olive oil

Blend together the flour, eggs and oil. Work it for 5 mins, then leave to rest.

Roll out until thin or machine roll at least 6 times, then leave to dry for 10 mins before cutting into strips or lengths.

Cook for 2 or 3 mins. Fresh chopped oregano may be added as a garnish.

Chateaubriand

1 8 oz fillet steak
1 lb waxy potato
1 egg yolk

Peel, chop and cook the potato for 10 mins until cooked.

Brush the steak with a little oil and pan fry for 5 mins each side. Leave to rest for 5 mins.

Meanwhile cream the potato adding the egg yolk and pipe into shallow oven tray then grill for 5 mins under a hot grill until golden brown.

Serve with crème fraiche.

Oven Baked Potato in Chicken Sauce

2 lb potato (sliced thinly)
1 onion (if tolerated) cook well
1 tbsp sugar
1 pint chicken stock (homemade)

Layer the potato into a buttered greased shallow oven dish. Fry the onion for 5 mins, sprinkle the sugar onto the onion and cook for a further 5 mins.

Layer the onion on top of the potato, then a layer of potato and pour over the chicken stock.

Cook for 40 to 45 mins gas mark 5.

A little cream may be added when cooked.

Grilled Rainbow Trout

2 fillet of trout
crème fraiche

Place the fish under a preheated grill and cook
for 3 mins each side.

Heat up the crème fraiche in a small sauce pan

Plate up the fish and pour over the crème
fraiche.

Serve up with new potatoes and a crispy salad.

Salmon en Croute

2 fresh salmon fillets
1 packet filo pastry
1 oz butter
baking tray

Grease the tray with butter. Place on it the clean dry salmon fillets 3 inches apart.

Lay out the filo pastry and roll out until large enough to cover the fish and top and sides.

Brush each layer with a little melted butter.

Make a few cuts in the pastry and bake in a preheated oven for 20 mins gas mark 7 – 425°F.

Oven Roast Lamb & Vegetables

2 lamb chops or steaks
1 large carrot
1 large potato
2 sprigs of rosemary

Peel and quarter the potato and carrot, place on an oven proof shallow tray with the lamb and rosemary, brush with a little oil.

Place in a hot oven gas mark 5 for 30 mins. Then turn the vegetables and meat, cook for a further 10 mins.

Serve up with some crunchy broccoli.

French Fries & Steak with Caramelized Onion

1 8 oz fillet or rump steak
2 large potatoes
1 small onion
1 tbsp sugar
2 oz garden peas
oil for frying chips

Peel and chop the potato and cook in oil for 10 mins.

Pan fry the steak for 3 or 4 mins each side, then leave to rest on a plate. In the same pan fry off the onion for 5 mins, then add the sugar and cook for a further 3 mins.

Cook the peas for 3 mins in boiling water.

Cottage Pie

1 lb fresh minced beef or lamb
1 med onion (chopped)
1 med carrot (diced)
2 lb potato (chopped)
½ pint beef stock (homemade)

Boil the potato for 10 to 15 mins until cooked.

Chop and cook the onion gently in a large pan for 5 mins stirring constantly. Then add the meat to the onion, cook for a further 10 mins until the meat is brown – keep stirring. Then add the carrot and beef stock. Simmer gently for 10 mins.

Place the meat into a shallow oven dish with the stock. Cream the potato and layer on top. Place in a hot oven gas mark 5 for 1 hour.

Bean Casserole

1 onion
10 oz butter beans (pre-soaked)
1 cup of chicken stock (homemade)
1 glass of white wine
4 oz single cream

Pan fry the chopped onion in a large pan for 5 mins. Add the butterbeans, chicken stock and wine. Simmer gently for 10 mins.

Add a handful of garden peas and simmer for 3 mins.

Stir in the single cream for 1 min.

A lovely warming winter food.

Potato Gratin

2 large waxy potatoes
¾ pint milk
¼ pint cream (single)

Peel, chop and cook the potato for 8 to 10 mins until half cooked.

Strain the potato and slice into half inch slices. Then layer into a gratin dish, pour over the milk and cream.

Place into a hot oven and cook for 40 to 45 mins gas mark 5.

A little grated cheese may be added on top halfway through the cooking.

Risotto

4 oz or 1 cup of Basmati Rice
6 shallots
4 oz garden peas
1 pint of chicken stock (homemade)

Finely chop and fry the shallots in a little oil – in a large frying pan for 5 mins. Add the rice to the onion and stir well. Cook gently for 2 mins.

Add the chicken stock cover with a lid and cook for 45 mins until all the liquid has been absorbed.

5 mins before the end of the cooking time, add the garden peas.

Serve up with some crusty bread.

Chicken in Mushroom Sauce with Puff Pastry

1 large chicken breast or 2 legs
6 oz mushrooms (quartered)
1 oz butter
1 oz flour
1 cup milk
12 oz packet puff pastry

Cook the chicken for 10 to 15 mins – set aside.
Place the butter, flour and milk into a small
saucepan and whisk together. Bring to boil and
simmer for 5 mins.

Chop up the chicken and combine with the
mushrooms in the white sauce. Leave to cool.

Roll out the pastry to about 12" by 15" into two
pieces for the top and the bottom, spoon the
chicken and mushrooms into the pastry. Brush
all around the end of the pastry with egg wash –
then layer the top of the pastry and seal all around.
Egg wash the top of the pastry and make 3 or 4
cuts in it.

Preheat oven to gas mark 6, cook for 45 mins
until brown and crispy.

Barbecued Lamb Steaks

Brush the lamb steaks with olive oil mixed with chopped herbs and rosemary and cook for 5 mins on each side. Serve up on a bed of rice.

Or

Pan fry the lamb with fresh sprigs of rosemary and whole button mushrooms. Serve with a crispy salad.

Or

Marinate the lamb in olive oil and mixed herbs and grill with aubergine, courgette and baked potato.

B.B.Q. Steaks

Sirloin or rump, brush with oil and cook for 3 mins each side. Serve up with a mixed salad and crusty bread.

Smoked Haddock, Leek and Mushroom Pie

2 oz butter
1 large leek (washed and chopped)
10 oz smoked haddock
6 oz milk
¼ pint crème fraiche
6 oz mushroom (chopped)
8 oz puff pastry
1 egg beaten (to glaze)

Cook the leek in 1 oz butter gently for 10 mins –
add a tablespoon of water if it dries out too
quickly during cooking.

Whilst the leek is cooking poach the haddock in
a large frying pan with milk for 5 mins. Remove
the fish from the milk and flake it into an oven
proof dish.

Fry the mushrooms in a little butter for 3 or 4
mins until golden brown.

Combine the leek and mushroom to the haddock
then add the crème fraiche.

Divide the pastry in half and roll out one half on
a floured board to about 10 inches round.

Place onto a greased shallow oven tray. Pile on the haddock and mushrooms. Leave a one inch space all around the edges of the pastry. Egg wash the edge of the pastry.

Roll out the second pastry and place on top. Seal and crimp the edge, egg wash the top of the pastry then crisscross with a sharp knife. Make about six cuts.

Preheat the oven to gas mark 6 – 200°C - cook for 35 to 40 mins until crispy and golden brown.

Serve with new potato and garden peas.

Chicken with Mozzarella

1 large chicken breast (boneless)
1 oz butter 50 gm
2 tbsp oil
1 ball of buffalo mozzarella

Cut the chicken breast in half lengthways. Fry gently in the oil and butter for 5 mins each side.

Transfer the chicken to a foil covered grill and spread over evenly the mozzarella, on each side of the chicken flat side up.

Cook under a hot grill for 3 or 4 mins until the cheese melts.

Serve up with crispy salad and baked potato.

Savoury Meat Balls & Coriander

1 lb lean minced beef
1 bunch of coriander
1 pint of beef stock (homemade)
1 cup of rice

Place the minced beef into a dish. Finely chop the coriander leaves and mix together with the meat. Then divide the mince into small balls.

Heat the beef stock in a large frying pan, when hot drop in the meat balls. Cook for 10 to 15 mins until cooked.

Cook the rice in one pint of boiling water for 8 mins.

Serve up the meat balls on the bed of rice and spoon over a little of the beef stock.

Italian Style Lamb Casserole

1 lb lean lamb (cubed)
2 tbsp flour (plain)
1 tbsp oil
2 red onions chopped (if tolerated)
1 courgette (chopped) (thick slices)
4 large tomatoes – home grown (chopped)
½ pint stock or water
2 sprigs of rosemary (chopped)
1 tbsp sugar
4 oz mushrooms

Coat the lamb in the flour. Heat the oil and seal the lamb for 5 mins. Add the onion, leek, courgette, tomato, rosemary and sugar. Add the stock and bring to boil. Cover with a lid and cook in a preheated oven for 1½ hours gas mark 4.

Remove the lid, stir and add the mushrooms. Cook for 30 mins.

Beef Bourguignon

1 lb sirloin steak
1 pint beef stock (homemade)
1 glass red wine
½ lb shallots
4 oz mushroom
1 tsp mixed herbs

Seal and brown the meat in a frying pan in a little oil for 5 mins. Then place into a casserole dish. Cook the shallots in the same pan for 5 mins. Then add them to the meat. Add the stock, wine and mixed herbs to the casserole, add the mushrooms, stir well and cover with lid

Cook in a hot oven, middle shelf, for 2 hours gas mark 4. Stir once or twice during cooking.

Spaghetti with Oregano

4 oz dry spaghetti
1 tsp oregano
1 oz cheese (low salt) grated

Cook the pasta in a pan of boiling water for 5 to 8 mins (test). Drain the pasta – return to pan, add the oregano – stir well.

Plate up and sprinkle on the grated cheese and toss in.

This dish would also be nice with the savoury meat balls.

Pasta

12 oz flour
3 large eggs

Sieve the flour onto a clean board. Make a well in the centre. Then break in the eggs. Gradually work the flour into the eggs to make a dough.

Knead for 10 mins. Set aside, cover and leave to rest for 1 hour.

Roll out with a rolling pin or pasta machine until thin enough to cut into strips.

To cook place in boiling water and cook for 3 or 4 mins.

Sea Bass Stuffed with Fresh Herbs

1 lb Sea Bass (cleaned)
Herbs – mint, basil, marjoram – tbsp each
chopped finely
75 ml olive oil

Make 6 or 7 cuts into the sea bass and fill with
the herbs mixed in oil.

Place the fish under a hot grill and cook each
side for 5 mins.

Serve with a green salad.

Grilled Rainbow Trout

2 fillets of rainbow trout
Crème fraiche

Place the fillet under a hot grill and cook for 3 mins each side.

Heat up the crème fraiche in a small saucepan.

Plate up and pour over the crème fraiche.

Serve with new potato and crusty bread or salad.

Beef Stew in Beer

1 lb lean stewing meat
½ lb shallots (peeled)
1 pint beer (stout)

Place the meat into a casserole dish with the shallots and beer. Place into the middle shelf in oven cook for gas mark 5 for one hour. Stir then lower to gas mark 4 for a further 2 hours.

Serve up with cabbage and carrots

Or

Baked potato brushed with oil and placed on the shelf around the casserole dish one hour before the casserole is cooked.

Pot Roasted Chicken

3 lb whole chicken (fresh)
2 lb potato (if tolerated)
small cabbage
1 tbsp oil

Place the chicken in an ovenproof dish with lid and cook for 2 hours basting at least once halfway through cooking.

Peel, chop and boil the potato for 5 mins strain off the water. Brush with oil and roast in the oven for about 45 mins until crispy.

Chop and cook the cabbage for 6 to 8 mins.

Serve up the chicken and vegetables pouring over a little chicken stock.

Cool the rest of the chicken stock take off any fat and store the stock in ice cube trays for soups or casseroles.

Marinated Grilled Lamb

1 leg spring lamb
2 tbsp olive oil
1 bunch of rosemary (chopped)

Mix together the olive oil and rosemary and pour over the lamb rubbing into the lamb then leave to marinate for 1 or 2 hours.

Preheat grill, remove the marina by patting dry with kitchen towel.

Cook under the grill for 10 to 15 mins turning halfway through the cooking time. Lower the heat if it cooks too fast.

Serve up with your favourite vegetables.

Bean sprouts with Mushrooms

1 onion (if tolerated)
6 oz mushrooms (sliced)
10 oz fresh bean sprouts

Finely chop the onion and cook for 8 to 10 mins until just changing colour.

Add the mushrooms to the onion and cook for 3 mins.

Then add the bean sprouts stirring continuously for 3 mins. A little water may be added if needed.

Plate up - a light supper dish.

Chicken Fricassee

1 3lb chicken (jointed)
1 onion (chopped)
1 celery stalk (chopped)
1 pint chicken stock (homemade)
A bouquet garni

Place the chicken, onion, celery, chicken stock and bouquet garni into a large pan with a lid. Simmer gently for 1½ hours then take out the bouquet garni.

A little cream may be added when cooked.

Or

You can also oven cook it for 1½ hours gas mark 5.

A great winter warming food.

Cauliflower au Gratin

1 cauliflower
1 oz butter
1 oz flour
2 oz cheese (low salt) (grated)
1 cup of milk

Wash and tail the cauliflower cook for 10 to 15 mins (test).

Place the butter, flour and milk into a small saucepan bring together by whisking – simmer gently for 5 mins stirring all the time.

Then add the grated cheese and simmer for 1 minute

Strain the cauliflower, plate up and pour over the lovely cheese sauce.

Meat Loaf

1 lb lean minced beef
1 leek (finely chopped)
1 bunch of parsley (finely chopped)
1 egg (beaten)
1 carrot (grated)

Mix the meat, leek and carrot in a bowl add the parsley and egg, combine together.

Place all the mixture into a greased meatloaf tin and cover with tin foil.

Bake in a hot oven for 1 hour gas mark 6. Take off the foil for the last 15 mins.

Serve hot or cold with a crispy salad.

Quiche Lorraine

6 oz shortcrust pastry
1 small red onion (sliced)
Small broccoli (florets)
¼ lb mushrooms (sliced)
2 eggs
½ pint milk

Line a 7" flan tin with the pastry. Cook the onion for 10 mins. Add the mushroom to the onion, cook for a further 3 mins.

Boil the broccoli for 5 mins.

Beat the eggs and add to the milk. Place the onion, mushroom and strained broccoli onto the pastry.

Pour over the egg and milk through a sieve

Bake in a hot oven for 45 mins gas mark 5.

Salmon Steaks

1 or 2 salmon steaks
2 tbsp oil
1 oz butter

Heat a frying pan with the oil and butter, when hot place in the salmon steaks, skin side down – cook for 5 mins basting continuously.

Serve up on a bed of crispy salad, lettuce, cucumber, diced celery and carrot.

Add a warm roll.

Delicious.

Breakfast on Brunch

Cottage cheese
Lettuce, salad etc...
Mellon
Pecan nuts
Pear

Slice the melon and pear arrange around a plate.
Place some crispy salad leaves in the centre and
top with cottage cheese.

Sprinkle over the pecan nuts.

Breakfast Choices

Eggs

Poached	Toast
Boiled	Pears
Scrambled	Melon
Omelette	Pancakes
Honey	
Tomatoes (home grown)	

Tomato may be added to omelette, as can low salt cheese or mushrooms.

Porridge Oats

1 cup of oats to one cup of milk into a Pyrex dish and microwave for 2 mins on high. Stir, then check to see if it needs a little more milk – stir then cook for one more minute – top with honey or sugar.

Pancakes

2 oz flour
1 egg
1 cup of milk
1 oz butter for cooking

Whisk together the flour, egg and milk until a smooth texture.

Heat a frying pan, add a little butter, when hot ladle in the pancake mixture.

Cook for about 2 mins each side. The mixture should make 3 or 4 pancakes.

Top with honey or sugar.

Bread and Butter Pudding

8 slices of white bread
2 oz butter
6 eggs
2 oz brown sugar
2 oz sultana
1 pint milk

Grease an ovenproof dish with some of the butter and butter the bread with the rest of it.

Cutting off the crust, line the dish with the bread, base and sides. Sprinkle the sultanas and sugar onto the bread and continue to layer bread and sultana.

Whisk together the eggs and milk. Sieve it over the bread and sultanas.

Bake in a hot oven for 40 to 45 mins gas mark 4.

Rice Pudding

One cup of small grain rice in a pan of boiling water (2 cups.) Simmer gently for 5 or 10 mins until most of the water has been absorbed.

Then place the rice in an ovenproof dish. Cover with a pint of milk and a tablespoon of sugar. Stir well, add a few knobs of butter on top.

Cook for 1½ hours gas mark 4.

Egg Custard

4 eggs to a pint of milk. Beat together. Sieve into an ovenproof dish. Add a tablespoon of sugar and stir

Cook for 1 hour or until set on gas mark 4.

Victoria Sandwich Cake

4 oz butter
4 oz sugar (caster)
4 oz flour (self raising)
2 eggs

Cream together the butter and sugar until a light mixture forms. Beat the eggs and add slowly to the mixture. Sieve in the flour and fold in. A spot of milk may be added if too stiff.

Grease a 9" round cake tin, spoon in the mixture. Bake in a preheated oven gas mark 5 for 25 to 30 mins.

Small Sponge Cakes

3 eggs
3 oz sugar (caster)
3 oz flour (self raising)

Whisk or beat the eggs and sugar until thick and creamy. Sieve in the flour and fold in lightly.

Spoon into individual paper cups.

Bake for 15 mins in a preheated oven gas mark 5 – 375°F.

Carrot Cake

4 oz butter
3 large eggs
8 oz flour (self raising)
4 oz brown sugar
1 large carrot (grated)
3 oz raisins (optional)

Cream together butter and sugar – add the eggs and beat.

In a large bowl sieve the flour add the fruit, the carrot and mix together. Combine together with the butter and eggs, if too stiff add a tablespoon of milk.

Grease a 9" cake tin with a loose bottom. Bake in a preheated oven middle shelf gas mark 5 for 30 mins. Then lower to gas mark 4 for 30 mins.

Test the centre of the cake, if still moist give it another 5 mins. Turn out to cool on a wire rack.

Please do go on to try different foods and create your own recipe But! Do remember to use only fresh food Good luck and best wishes

Eileen Murphy